Chasing Rainbows

To my brother, Joe for his help and advice in difficult times; life-long friends Dave and Chris.

Dorothy, my wife and best pal; for criticism, corrections and patience. My eternal thanks.

Chasing Rainbows

Richard Maitland

THE CHOIR PRESS

First published in the United Kingdom in 2018 by
The Choir Press

ISBN 978-1-911589-75-4

Contents

Short Poems

Afterwards

With hormones surging to a peak,
Romantic Love was quite unique.
Yet Innocence and make-believe
boosted my faith and joie de vivre.
And so I magicked a pleasure dome
that she and I could both call home.
But even as I mused, pretending,
all was coming to an ending.

For fantasies were swept away
when she recalled her holiday.
Two weeks, she said. A little while.
Retiring then, behind a smile.
My friends said, no. Don't let her go.
But Trust's not only there for show.
So I ignored their urgent pleas;
trusting our love had guarantees.

And now her holiday is done,
there's really no comparison
between the girl who went away
and then returned the other day.
For now, when she and I are near,
the difference is all too clear.
That faraway look in haunted eyes
reveals too many hidden lies.

And cupid lips that once were bliss;

as apple-skinned

as a Judas kiss.

Always One

For 'art' we need an artist,
it doesn't matter who.
So let's forget the labels,
and call that someone 'you'.
It does away with gender,
Nature's dividing line;
and substitutes 'Equality'
that state we rate divine.

Equality. Equality.
It starts with Revolution;
and seems to be,
for you and me,
the only right solution.
But when there is a multitude
it has to be divided
and jobs accorded not at will
but skilfully one-sided.

So as of need, numbers impede
Equality's foundation.
And bureaucrats find caveats
to boost their glorification.

But there's always one above the rest
who doesn't have to be the best.
But rises upwards through the ranks
without the help of guns and tanks
yet somehow, all his peers outflanks

to reach the very crest.

Atlas's Arms

Letters on paper
inflate themselves
when gathered up in meaning.
Emotions stir,
and start to purr:
the prelude to feline preening.

But action's never
a certainty;
that Joker's out of season.
An easy mark,
without the spark
or ruthlessness of Reason.

It never veers
from left to right,
nor stumbles on approach.
But hits its target
every time,
eluding self-reproach.

For Science and Reason
are Atlas's arms;
known all over the planet.
Stronger than Faith,
though lacking its charms;

and believers
with hearts of granite.

Back To Basics

To matters scatological,
I've never been inclined.
Despite an oath to Hippocrates,
I also read, and signed.
With examinations ended,
my Doctorate commended,
no sudden urge could make me break a rule.
But without being vague,
I'd rather risk plague;
than examine a patient's stool.

No incident's filed,
but once as a child;
walking back home with dad.
I cried and cried; until inside
my Mum said: 'Nothing's that bad.'

But by face I could tell,
she was smelling that smell;
the smell of my latest mischance.
When in comes Ben, stirring again;

"O sister dear,
please don't come near
for I fear
you have

pooped in your pants."

Barbarossa

Ghosts in the mind assert their presence
with angry words and fits of rage.
Affecting us all in adolescence,
but still as crabbéd in old age.
Ghosts are always abstract nouns,
never referring to anything real:
soldiers, sailors or circus clowns.
Fruit like bananas, we need to peel.

But words like Hate, Love, and Beauty,
lacking referents everywhere.
Words such as State, Obedience, Duty,
denoting values citizens share.
Yet though essential to life and living,
these ghosts have powers beyond our ken.
Because they're grim and unforgiving
when times start changing once again.

Some poets are prophets; and Heine could see
that the Cross of Christ was a fading power
in northern lands where spirits were free.
For who could resist the hammer of Thor,
after centuries of shepherds and lambs?
Or loving the neighbour whom you deplore,
and obeying suggestions from obvious shams?

Abstract nouns filled Hitler's head
with Communism stamped as vile.
Yet he made a pact with Joe the Red,
then broke his word, as was his style.
Attacking with millions and millions of men,
and planes and tanks and guns galore,
he soon had thousands of soldiers in pens.

Believing too soon, he'd won the war
with a sudden, successful beginning.

Because convinced he had the Will;

a ghost that wouldn't be winning.

Bedtime

Big Brother's fixed in every head
filtering information.
Watching while we eat our bread,
because that is his vocation.
Guardian of all both loved and lost:
Gaoler and warder beside.
Stiffer than any real Jack Frost
filled with formaldehyde.

"Orders is orders." You'll hear him say,
the moment he's decided.
And from then on there's no delay;
though his choice may be misguided.

He's not all there at the best times,
and frequently causes us trouble,
with silly tricks and pantomimes
where cauldrons boil and bubble.

So who is he, this bossy guy
who's watching all we do?
Cyclops with his single eye?
Some tough old buckaroo?

He's none of those, as you may have guessed;
but someone else instead.
And he, like me, must have his rest:

So off we go,
to bed.

Bits And Pieces

We are who we are when living at home,
known by our given name.
But, when with friends, formality ends,
and all of us suffer the same.
For Richard is Dick, or Ritchie, or Rick;
and Frederick is Freddie or Fred.
Elizabeth's Liz, Lisa or Beth,
Betty or sometimes Bess,
Margaret's Maggie, Peggy or Mags,
Jessica's Jessie, or Jess.
When out of the cage,
some nicknames enrage,
but they might set a crown on one's head.

In Infant School it doesn't apply,
we are who we are once again.
Answering questions truthfully:
not hungry for future gain.
Unsure of ourselves, without any measure;
swamped by the constant din.
Newcomers all, short and tall.
Losers; and those who'll win.

Secondary school, adheres to the rule,
given names fall away,
and are quickly replaced by others;
depending what's on display.

For anything odd is a target
attracting attention at once.
A lisp, a lapse, a stutter
will trigger a snap response.
Gingered by hoots of laughter,
and shrieks if the foggy reacts,
unaware he'll exceed them by millions,
as master of figures and facts.
An international banker,
cosy with Heads of State.
Director of multiple companies,
though still of bantamweight.

'Know Thyself' said the Oracle at Delphi;
as a counter to human caprices.
And those who heard followed each word;

while the rest

stayed in bits and

pieces.

Bodies

When bodies meet
they're incomplete,
lacking all dimension.

And so surprised,
or ill-advised,
it never gets a mention.

Boomerang Boy

What would you do if the man at the door,
a six foot bruiser, expression grim,
pushed you aside and declared your house,
and all its contents belonged to him?
Would you fight like a tiger
defending her own?
Or collapse in a heap
and lie there and groan?

It's not the loss of a thousand bricks,
although they too deserve some praise.
But treasures inside, long kept with pride;
mementoes of much happier days.
Corporal Kennedy D.L.I.
with lots of ginger hair to comb.
Smiling broadly for mum and dad,
so many miles away from home.
Yet looking around, he couldn't believe
the hundreds of miles travelled so far.
The church, the pub, the corner shops:
so familiar, so bizarre.
The barracks too, though out of bounds,
were duplicates of those he'd known.
Discipline and Sergeants' orders;
the British army's foundation stone.

What are we doing here, he wondered,
though there it lay before his eyes.
No enemies threatened this peaceful country.
What was the point of the exercise?
Only the Colonel would be in the know,
though he, old soldier, was well-equipped.
Completely ignoring the lesser ranks,
when stalking the barracks; alert, tight-lipped.

The territory was ours all right.
Christian churches always full.
Bibles present in every house,
instead of the former enemy skull.
English spoken, and taught at school.
Bare breasts now covered. (*Life's downs and ups.*)
Former chiefs now wearing suits,
and drinking tea from china cups.

It was only their colour that let them down.
Black faces gave the game away.
Mixed marriages helped, but not that much.
And yet we underlined '*fair play*'.
It wasn't so much hypocrisy
that kindled doubt in Kennedy's brain.

But having travelled around the world,
here he was
back home

again.

—◦◉◦—

Casanova At Large

Do the girls I courted think of me now
when forty or fifty years are gone?
Do they sometimes lie awake in bed,
wishing they'd married me instead
of choosing another one?

Of course, it's possible some have succumbed
to charms and promises aimed to please.
Both the ploys of jesting Death
to rob them of their wheezing breath
and bring them onto their knees.

And even more the Disappointed
whose former dreams no longer reign;
because Reality, unexpected
crudely, rudely interjected;
sealing darkness in their brains.

'They are but few among the many',
a fellow graduate once mused.
'Check on the web and you'll observe
they follow a bell shaped curve,
that's seldom, if ever, abused.

He was wrong, of course; and now in gaol
I'm serving time; five years in all.
Five long years still trickling by;
leaving me pondering: Why? Why? Why?
Why didn't I recall?

He wasn't wrong, he wasn't right.
He'd always been somewhere between.
Convincing? Yes, with a silver tongue.
As much the same as I'd begun:

Bold as brass,

and evergreen.

Chasing Rainbows

Rainbows are at the very core
of everything I write.
Like Edgar, and his 'Nevermore'
wrapping his poems up tight.

For they abound in mythologies
of peoples far and wide.
But vary a lot in meaning,
being diversified.

In Genesis, a rainbow appears
after the world-wide flood.
As a covenant made with believers,
tired of the shedding of blood.

As a Norseman's bridge to the heavens
or a messenger from the sky;
An archer's bow or a serpent.
Rainbows will always comply.

Omnipresent everywhere,
thanks to water and light.
And yet, as visitors casually rare,
to spoil all childish delight.

And so I wonder if Edgar Poe
once followed the very same path.
And, up above, is looking down;

enjoying a graveyard laugh.

Comfort Zone

I love to see a rainbow,
a rainbow in the sky.
And, as a child, asked questions;
eager for any reply.

Some said they were an omen;
but that was all they knew.
Some said, a bridge to heaven.
And others had no clue.

"Why don't you ask your teacher?"
My dad said with a grin.
"That's what she's been trained for,
despite her discipline."

I knew that he was having fun,
but asked her later on.
*"Wait behind at playtime,
when the other children have gone ..."*

I told her what I'd learned so far;
she listened, to all I said.
Then took my little hand in hers
and gently stroked my head.

"When the Sun shines through the rainclouds,
there's colour in the air.
And the whole world is rejoicing
with rainbows everywhere.

There to give us pleasure;
and darkness to dispel.

Underlying His promise:

His Promise – "All is well."

Coronation Time

Being bored
when you're alone
signals too much
testosterone.
Too many hormones
urging you on,
although you're nearly
ninety-one.

To slow the world
when Time is flitting,
it's common sense
to take up knitting.
It calms the nerves
and eases tension
when Concentration
is in ascension.

But if you're filled
with indignation,
I recommend
some meditation.
The Buddha's cure
for self-vexation,
that lasts awhile
because it's Asian.

But for millions
of those who pray,

this is the true,
and only
Way.

A conquest lasting
years and years,
where Nirvāna waits
for him who dares.

It may seem
I'm imperious,
or bordering on
delirious.
But humour won't
be serious
if you crown it

with a smile.

Counting The Days

Days are different, quite unique;
happening seven times a week.
All individual, but all the same,
and we're the only ones to blame;
by way of Capitalistic bent.
(although a few were quite content.)

For then the Church was still around,
its power and influence profound;
having established a holy day
on which the peasants had to pray.
And Sunday bells conditioned all
as years went by, to heed their call.

Yet Anglo-Saxon gods were hale
in days of the week which still prevail.
Maun, Tui, Woden and Thor;
Freya, and Sunne; but Saturn, ignore.

For he's the joker in the pack.
A extra Anglo-Saxons lacked.
The god of Time whose Nature's sour,
knowing our name, and final hour.
Indifferent; from noble stock,

who's never had to watch

the clock.

Cross-Wired?

Waking up we make connections
with a world we've left behind.
It's not the same, but not much different:
even for those who are misaligned.
For senses sometimes take a turn
and ignore the usual links.
And may have done since childhood days,
entirely content to be out of sync.

So those agreeing about what they're seeing
count themselves as being 'straight',
and those who view colours when music plays,
are the synesthetes who deviate.

Letters and figures can also be triggers
transforming the world as we know it.
As artists have shown, we all have a zone,
though there's seldom an urge to show it.

And if you want Reality,
consider how locusts live out a day.
Some of them staying solitary,
while millions together go storming away.
But tickle back legs and both will change
one into the other.
For two-in-one is Nature's way
of linking sister to brother.

Yet economists speak of the 'average man'
who doesn't really exist at all;
being only an abstract construction,
and nothing like the Berlin Wall.

Which once was real, but now is not:
though habits may obtain.
But passports, mirrors, family, friends
don't know the 'you' alive in your brain.
And if they could, would it do any good?
For Life itself is a mystery;
and miniature version's have little chance
of acting any differently.

Yet some have crossed the shadow-line,
by using text as a way to disarm
their readers of complacency;
while still allowing enough to alarm.
The gloss in 'The Rime of The Ancient Mariner'
disrupting reading, now and again.
The imagery of opium visions
where time and space discard their reins.

So leave us alone without direction.
Ships adrift in a cosmic sea.
Starlight shining from our innards:

and never devoid

of

bel esprit.

Dark Times

Light is the life conceived in darkness
questioning, questioning why it is.
Dark the unknown, we seek to conquer:
by assuming we have the right to quiz.
One is Ego, the other, Id,
as Freudians deigned to tell us so.
Though I prefer the single word;
chiaroscuro.

A single word it may well be,
although portmanteau serves it fine.
Fusing the two together
into the one design.
Film Noir wasn't a genre,
but a film making style.
Taking a lead from *chiaroscuro,*
proving itself so versatile.
Experimentation was the key
as cinematographers found.
Lighting changing from front to side,
adding depth to actors, props and ground.

A dramatic story was essential;
peppered with sex, murder and crime.
Filled with tension, danger, betrayal:
all of them working overtime.
A mother's desperate love for her daughter,
so totally selfish and hard of heart.
Prepared to kill to get her way;
her singular wish, a life apart.

An insurance man who commits a murder
for a femme fatale, who'd done the same
to her husband's wife, then married him;
but now regretting a life too tame.

Dark times indeed, and not for us
who had to wait until of age.
Though Horror comics, deftly swapped,
always enjoyed our patronage.
I remember a story in an old folks' home
where inmates, starved, were never fat.
And only one had a visitor;
cheerfully welcomed, although a rat.
Yet rules were rules, and well respected
for children had to be protected.

How I welcomed reaching sixteen,
and old enough to pass their test.
Secure in a job, after leaving school,
with manhood nearly manifest.
Old enough now to reach my goal:
admitted to films that made me feel whole.
As if an actor playing a part,
because overwhelmed by the power of art.

Urged by emotions, heartfelt, yet fierce;

and the faultless perfection of *'Mildred Pierce'*

—◦◌◦—

Dead Reckoning

They used to call it living,
and now I'm dead, I see
just what it meant to others;
though not a tad to me.

They used to call me horrid names,
and make my life a misery;
and so I killed myself one day
so they would let me be.

My mother called me, silly boy.
My dad leapt up in glee,
after hearing what I had done;
then kicked me on the knee.

It didn't hurt; not like before
when I had cried to ease the pain.
He simply stared, and then he smiled,
kicking me once again.

"Leave him alone. He's had enough."
My mother's voice commanded.
And dad sat down, shaking his head,
but doing as she demanded.
"He's telling the truth. Can't you see?
You're such a dunderhead.
No punishment can harm him now.
Our little boy

is dead."

Dedication

Ogden Nash made lots of cash
by writing poems that rhymed.
As money inflated,
he sat and created;
because he was that way inclined.

With a family to feed,
there was always a need
for burgers and tea by the ton.
Cakes baked by the score;
then, afterwards, more.
The feasting had just begun.

A woman's life, easier now,
with both sides respecting the marriage vow.
And a housewife's day now sweet, not sour;
with scientist and engineer
delivering servants not too dear,
all fed by electrical power.

A life that others also craved,
but couldn't get unless they saved:
and that, was balderdash.
For stocks and shares at an all time high,
suddenly tumbled and waved goodbye
with a devastating crash.

And businesses fell like dominoes;
while Governments dithered; one man rose
to give himself some air.
A sheet of paper in his hand.
A messenger from fairyland.

Another poem to share.

Directions

Poetry's prose without a rhyme.
(Poetical licence is not a crime.)
Usually placed at the end of a line;
depending on the weather.

By which I don't mean rain or snow,
but whether adrenalin's high or low.
When Life's saying yes; instead of no,
and everything's together.

Keeping in touch when far apart,
and waiting for that magic start.
Bringing to birth a work of art,
by mixing words and feeling.

Surprising us by sleight of mind,
with this and that so intertwined
we'll never know what's there to find:

Or what the poet's

concealing.

Effectively Dead

Robots blessed with perfect balance;
can walk a tight-rope without a care.
Always polite, and never moody,
with no emotional burdens to bear.
To that extent they suit employers,
cutting outgoings considerably.
Needing no wages, consumables, training;
toilets, car parks, or breaks for tea.

Yet now and again need some attention,
self-repairing when there's a need.
And not until the shift is over
will human action intercede.
But even then it's done in comfort;
no spurting blood as used to be.
But swift exchange of damaged units,
and back to work immediately.

A binary system of one and nought
controls decisions throughout the day.
Electricity powers their actions:
Programs are orders they must obey.
No problems then for factory owners,
relaxing at ease on silver sands
of islands in the Caribbean;
where slaves had chains
on legs and hands.

Robots are slaves, but they don't know it.
And ignorance, bliss, as Shakespeare said.
Meaning of course, sentient beings:
not up-to-date tools,

effectively dead.

Everywhere Man

The Ancient Greeks figured it out;
doing away with the ground.
Falsifying Reality
to tap the power they had found.
Reason and Rationality
usurping both sham and sage,
but also diminishing what man was,
by enclosing him in a cage.

From animal to something more;
and all in a very short time.
Relatively speaking you'll understand;
with Plato their teacher, at prime.
But was he really that intent
on what would later come to be?
Or merely seeking religious light
to end uncertainty?

The answer's both because he'd scope
enough as a polymath,
to change direction as and when
and follow another path.
But stumbled into an abstract world
where labels outweighed the rest.

Until Aristotle took it in hand,
and straightened the arabesque.

Father And Sons

The body's
invisible
until a pain
stabs like a dagger
and raises Cain.

Out in the fields
to greet the Dawn.
Tilling the soil
because firstborn.
Marked as a slave
by God's command;
immune to death
by human hand.

Immune to death
but not travail.
In Jehovah's eyes
he is bound to fail.

Able's the man;
again and again.

And a body's
nobody;
if it
ain't got a

brain.

Fire And Ice

Fire and ice, the two extremes
of adolescence and old age.
Thinning blood, no prayer redeems.
Overheated hormonal rage.

One but many of those alone
who face confusion at the change.
Historically it's not unknown.
So why should sufferers think it strange?

In classrooms children sit and learn
subjects considered fitting.
For afterwards, they'll have to earn
their keep, while Time is flitting.

So far, so good.
But something's missing
that points the way to health.
No deliberate omission,
but the
sensible:

KNOW

THYSELF.

Freewheeling?

Everything's out in the open,
where once, it used to be closed.
The Internet
remains dead set
on seeing us all overdosed.

The entire world is changing,
becoming less urbane;
with figures replacing letters,
and swear words now germane.

How long has this been going on?
And why the sudden hurry?
We've been on Earth for many years,
but now are plagued with worry.

With Climate change, and populations
soaring into the ether.
The outlook's grim,
and chances slim
we'll ever get it together.

Once 'husband' meant: one owned a home,
and had nothing to do with marriage.
And if you understand this poem:

It may give much

to disparage.

Friendship

I didn't mean to hurt you,
nor act for selfish ends;
but to show the watching public
that you and I are friends.

For eyes see only surface,
and brains just need a nudge
to jump to false conclusions;
then play the hanging judge.

It's all interpretation,
we never know for sure
just what another's thinking;
prognostication's obscure.

And yet, though others are lost at sea,
on land, it's very plain to me.

A friend's a friend until the end,

and you, my friend

will always be.

Getting To Know You

"I've heard her cursing the *Führer*."
Matilda Grossmund said.
"And say life would be better
if someone shot him dead.
Of course she'd lost her husband
only the previous week.
But it's duty to report her,
so I thought I'd better speak."

In Russia, Alexi Barino
denounced the woman next door;
who'd lopped off her son's three fingers,
so he couldn't go to war.
They came and took the both of them
as examples to the rest.
While villagers stayed safely inside
without a thought expressed.

No-one informed on Bletchley Park.
Its secret lasted for years.
Though information topped the bill,
and exhaustion occasioned flares.
The first computer in the world
eventually proved its worth.
Exposing Nazi intentions,
and giving the Future birth.

All governments still gather facts
about their populations.
Not personal; but generic
and within strict limitations.
Though now all data has its price
and every bit has lots of bite.
For dinosaurs direct our lives
not knowing wrong from right.

And people worship at a screen
as once they did in Egypt's land.
Entangled again, and self-obsessed.
Clicking buttons on demand.
Until they've covered many pages
with secrets there for all to see.
Meeting new friends, but never thinking
they could be the end of me.

Information is what they're after,
the billionaires who run the show.
and sell it to the highest bidders;
manufacturers now in the know.
Their expertise has only one focus.
In the spotlight there you are
unaware of self-betrayal –

and destined for

the abattoir.

Getting Together

An author is invisible,
though present in every book.
And if you don't believe me,
surprise her by sneaking a look.
She's bound to be there somewhere,
but let's not to make a fuss.
For if you can't find her body,
there's always her animus.

Poets cunningly hide themselves
deep in forests of tropes.
Using similes or metaphors
to parade their hidden hopes.
And steer their readers skilfully towards
a catch they needn't kill.
Where understanding counts for all
yet still rewards them with a thrill.

The artist and his work of art,
whatever it may be;
is caught in a relationship
high in hyperbole.
But if successful, one's the other;
and two together can snuggle.
Inseparable, though still apart;

having brought to an end

the struggle.

Hail Caesar!

We value words for their meaning,
but that doesn't always apply.
For people have many reasons,
to put that assumption by.
They may be charged with emotion,
and hurting too much inside.
Determined to crush their tormentor
So what, if it's homicide?
Or maybe they're being deceptive,
concealing intent by disguise;
with forthrightness bearing the burden
at the head of a hundred lies.
For some people seeking advantage
is an almost delectable task.
And what makes it even more thrilling
is doing without a mask.

Masking ourselves is essential,
though no-one's there to report.
For we all hear voices inside us;
otherwise known as thought.
But also, hallucinations
occurring in overtaxed brains,
known as psychotic disorders
where delusion and chaos reigns.

Yet that is a life abnormal;
far from the world we've won,
apart from old Mother Nature:

having crossed the Rubicon.

Happy The Man

Happy the man who has a home
where he can sit and write a poem.
Balanced inside on gliding wings,
considering Life:
and other things.

How does he do it, day after day?
Surely he knows, without any play
Life becomes steadily duller and duller;
while balancing interests fills it with colour.

Yet those who walk the path alone
may find contentment of their own,
as children playing with friends unseen.
Until their parents intervene.

Believing all is for the best,
and once convinced, become obsessed;
while suffering from self-deceit.

Until we die,

Life's

incomplete.

How To Write A Poem

Beginning is the hardest.
But when that deed is done;
the darkest clouds are over,
making way for the Sun.
And though he's so much weaker
beginning his daily climb,
we must allow for senescence
and award him extra time.

For when he reaches his station,
his warmth will ease your plight.
So study each word you have written
until one of them leads to the light.
Consider its connotations,
and all that that study unveils.
Treasures so carefully hidden
in hundreds of fairytales.

Then follow that trail through the forest
though it vanishes now and then.
Eaten by birds for breakfast,
with never a single '*Amen*'.

So that is how to write a poem:
It may leave you aghast.

But mine's a deliberate omission:

Please, fashion your title

last.

In Days Of Old

Big Brother isn't watching you,
but shepherds have their sheep.
And as they baa, we baa-baa back
secrets we meant to keep.

In olden days, whatever our ways
acceptance was the norm.
A mixed-up crew,
some old, some new
all wore a uniform.
British we were,
both him and her,
whatever their colour or caste.
And year after year
prices were fair;
until one day the Chancellor said: "Blast!
Our gold reserves are far too low.
The Empire's drifting apart.
We've given all, but had to fall;
though not through loss of heart."

Today we seldom march in step,
and hide ourselves away.
Forgetting how we carried our flags
on the twenty fourth of May.
Children of Empire,
open to all.
So unprepared
for its final Fall.

In Others Words

When using words to communicate
we sometimes make a blunder.
And get from its recipient
such telephonic thunder

that shakes foundations long since laid,
we thought would last forever.
But must have been of lower grade,
despite my hubby's endeavour.

He tries his best and that's enough
for me, a wife of forty years.
When scoundrels boast and strut their stuff
like that Doctor of Moliere's.

When asked why opium induced sleep,
he pondered a while in fever.
Until at last, after thinking deep,
he replied:
"Because of its

virtus dormitiva."

In other words, a repetition
from a doctor who's more of

a politician.

Indian Giver

When I awoke in '47
and pulled the curtains apart;
lying outside was a gift from heaven,
exploding my brain, thrilling my heart.

The world had changed by God's command
and everything was new.
No more the long-neglected land,
that strangely, was taboo.

I gulped my bread and jam at speed,
while mother shook her head.
But no one now could intercede;
and out from the house I sped.

Boys and girls were everywhere,
little children once again.
With snowballs flying through the air,
as if on a daisy chain.

Running and chasing each other around,
becoming more excited;
some of us falling to the ground,
though quickly re-united.

Until we heard our mother's call
and hurried without delay.

Knowing her dinners were best of all:

And **She**, never took them away.

Internal Disturbances

It sometimes gets too much for me
doing the things I do.
Although I've managed, as you can see,
without any ballyhoo.
I blame the others for letting me down,
old friends I've known for years.
Newer arrivals after my crown:
who Jealousy always ensnares.

My job description doesn't exist;
though the workload's always been grim.
There's no routine; it's been dismissed
and all because of him.
A bit of this and a bit of that;
Jack of all trades that's me.
Though born a proletariat
I've still got my Ph.D.

And yet I can't advance at all
because I know that he is there.
Set in his ways, still having the gall
to take control. It isn't fair.
He's older of course, and stills opines
that old-fashioned values obtain.
And being a reptile, pooh-poohs my designs

to spite a superior brain.

Intruders

Emotions are amateurs on the stage,
but having made it, rant and rage.
Determined to show, by sheer excess,
dramatic skills they don't possess.
While others seek to understate
the parts they play, and appreciate
an audience already au fait
with theatrical traits and the odd cliché.

Comparing the two, it seems as if
the first is dangling over a cliff;
from where below, white arms invite,
mermaids waiting to give delight.
While tothers with greater self-control,
convinced they see the picture whole,
have quite another perspective,
and one that's more protective.

But as the stage is in my head,
emotion is the devil I dread.
For after all, I'm middle-class;
retired and cognizant life must pass.
Contented in my private space,
without a thought that's out of place.
Until intruders chance to call
and very quickly end it all.

"The world's a stage."

As Shakespeare said:

But not when darkness usurps one's head.

Kên

Keep still my mountain, keep still.
But not forever and ever.
You'll move when it's time to move,
but for now, dismiss all endeavour.
And contemplating balance
reflect awhile, apart.
For only a man with a straightened back
can achieve a quiet heart.

Restlessness is a common curse
triggered by nerves in the spine.
But quietude's the other half
of a mammal's basic design.
It's written as a hexagram
where bottom and top are the same;
each trigram negating the other,
though both are still its aim.

The Book of Changes is more than a book;
it's the wisdom of three thousand years.
That takes as its premise an ordered whole;
a cosmos, it never outwears.

So cast your coins and move the heavens;
no longer so far apart.

For only a man with a straightened back

can achieve a quiet heart.

Letting Go

My mother used to say to me:
"Don't do that. Everyone's looking!'
It cured me of my *bonhomie*
because she took no brooking.
And even alone, without her there;
when friends returned to laugh and play.
I waited, nervously aware;
that she might chance to lose her way.

But then an offer to sing on stage
put fire inside my belly.
What better place for an anchorage;
even with legs of jelly?
So told my mum, who answered, hum;
grinding her teeth together.
Then poked the fire, about to expire,
while mumbling; you and your blether.

The man describing Fred Astaire
"Can't sing. Can dance a little."
Must have been around somewhere,
though equally noncommittal.

But why blame him? When we're offstage
and now it's *quid pro quo?*
Let's give the Truth some leverage.

For all her life

she never let go.

Life

One little female, pregnant again;
covered with slime, emerged into rain.
Big drops of water washing her clean
to start a new life in the blue and green.

On land at last, though still not free
of her mighty mother, the surging sea.
One little female, determined still
to bend the Future to her Will.

A whole new world, as yet unknown,
where she could live, but not alone.

Living With The Dead

A broken heart led me to art
one bleak December day.
As I limped into the library
with a book, and fine to pay.
Ms Armitage was on the desk
and shook her tight-lipped head.
"That's a charge of one pound twenty."
"That's fine by me." I said.

She stared at me, but didn't smile,
and with our business concluded.
Picked up the book that she'd put down
as soon as I had intruded.
'*The Poems of Edgar Allan Poe*'
was the title on the cover.
I'd read '*The Raven*', but was there more
to help myself recover?

"Hope you don't mind," I apologised.
"But is he the poet who lost his wife?"
She raised her hazel eyes to mine,
"And loved her, the rest of his life."
Then quietly started reciting:
"*Helen, thy beauty is to me*
Like those Nicean barks of yore
That gently o'er a perfumed sea
The weary, way-worn wanderer bore
To his own native shore."

It hurried homeward to my heart,
and settled there to stay.
Such eloquence; such melodies,
could lead a man astray.

Not only men, I realised,
recovering my senses.
For now I saw her misted eyes,
were lowering defences.

No other customers stood in line
awaiting her attention;
And so I dared to speak once more,
but still with apprehension.

"My name is Edward: Edward Morse.
We've met each other before."
Gently smiling, she nodded her head.
"Would you like me to quote you more?"

And that was how it started;
my boldness beckoning Chance.
Two strangers finding their common ground,
that in time would lead to Romance.

And courtship, marriage, husband and wife;
from vinegar to sparkling wine.

A gift from one long in his grave:

whose art caused love to shine.

Making Noises – The Lyrebird

It doesn't fly, although a bird.
But hear it once and you'll have heard
cacophonies unreal.
Chain saws, drills and car alarms
aren't celebrated for their charms;
yet can be some ordeal
when heard with songs learnt after birth,
(of which there's never any dearth)
but given away for free.
For copying is automatic,
though choices tend to be erratic:
they're there for mimicry.

Copying other birds at leisure;
though not entirely for the pleasure;
but more for the final effect.
The screech of an owl signalling danger
soon unsettles a hungry stranger,
who then must disconnect;

and leave his breakfast chirping gladly,
instead of sobbing, sobbing sadly
should fate had gone his way.
So lyrebirds protect their young,
and exercise their mother tongue
every single day.

Then spin the world a little faster,
and you will see a dancing master:
peaking at the breeding season.
From June to August males perform
dressed in a lyrebird's uniform.
All for the very same reason.

Four hours a day the male can sing,
each one attempting to be the King:
which females duly ignore.
Teasing the males although they know
the one who's going to be their beau;
that handsome troubadour.

But wait and wait, to urge him on,
and witness a phenomenon
rarely captured on screen.
Singing an ever present song,
the male bird never does anything wrong
to irritate his Queen.

Striding around his chosen plot,
as if the Lord of Camelot,
he spreads his lyre-like tail.
Increases volume on the beat,
until it's got a white-hot heat:
a beat that cannot fail.

But not this time, he's got it wrong;
For memories linger long in song;
and feelings won't shrink to nought.
Especially for females who're in the know:
Woman, vixen, heifer or doe.

Though not the emotional sort.

Nature Lesson

Opening eyes in the morning,
greeting another day.
Listen! A blackbird's singing.
I wish that he would stay.
To us, he brings such happiness
for there's pleasure in a song.
And so I lie contented;
happy I'm right, not wrong.

But thoughts are only fairytales,
and Fancies feed conceit.
Assuring us we're in control,
while masking self-deceit.
Romance and Rationalisation,
each on the opposite side,
are easily interconnected
when senses start to slide.

And living in the Present
is living in the Past,
and every painted flower's
no longer colourfast.
For Truth's a lie
we profit by,
escaping Nature's stings.
But all's complete,
when opposites meet.

That's why

my Blackbird

sings.

Nothing Mars

Not being oneself becomes the prize
we can attain, when in surprise,
ekstasis creates another me.
Another me, but still the same:
a pawn aware of the deadly game
in which we live without guarantee.

But if you're thinking, what the hell?
Be patient; I've a tale to tell
that's not the least distressing.
Transfiguration's what I mean.
A way whereby transition's seen;
with Mother Nature's blessing.

A peacock has a hundred eyes,
but think again; you'll realise
not all of them can see.
The statement's false, and yet is true;
for much depends on who is who,
and this hyperbole.

As sign and symbol lift us high
internally where we can fly
among surrounding stars.
Transformed by music, sculptures, plays,
and moved by ever-burgeoning praise
of songs on Blue Guitars.

Up there, where

nothing mars.

Now And Then

Here I sit, a lump of clay;
wondering why
I was made this way.
Jealous of those
who've reached their goal:
the sheer delight
of being whole.

But how have they achieved this prize?
By enslaving themselves,
and thinking it wise.
To me it's more of a total disaster;
being a slave, while still a master.

Spending each day repeating routines
when they should be at leisure.
Turning their bodies into machines,
but not for joy or pleasure.

Once it was all about the game,
fair play by those concerned;
and losing brought no lasting shame:
defeat would be returned.

Training was running, kicking stones,
and dribbling past your mates.
Taking a beating without any groans
and leaving the rest
to the Fates.

On Losing One's Keys

Most of the time they're never lost;
and what is worse, it's blatant,
They're hiding somewhere in the house
in keeping with their patent.
But since it's happened time and again
and I'm that wee bit older,
I've learnt a little self control
and give them a cold shoulder.

Relaxing in a cosy chair,
body and mind at ease,
Picturing all I've done today
like old Diogenes.
Link by link as in a chain,
from start until the end.
But still no sign of the vital clue
I need to comprehend.

If Reason's test is the very best
that Cynics entertain,
I must remark, all's still as dark
as once it was, again.
And so perhaps the darkness
that's always out of sight,
is blessed with a four-star memory,
that shines forever bright.

And knows the golden answer:

the only one

that's right.

On Writing Poems

This poem is not a confession;
nor was it meant to be.
Though critics give that impression,
citing it constantly.

Omitting all painters or writers,
who could be involved in the fraud;
being unscrupulous blighters
yet nevertheless, adored.

When Classism ruled the roost
and men adored machines.
Von Schlegel gave us all a boost
by using other means.

Romantic poets in the van,
renounced old explanations,
and brought to life organic man
for future generations.

But was that action really wise,
when it concerned emotions?
When Fear and Horror grew in size,
exciting wayward notions?

Notions like sexual desire,
and bodily connections.
Outlining details way past the wire:
But all of them:
only
confections.

One Of Many

Entropy and Evolution
will lead us all to dissolution
for, as of yet, there's no solution
to save us from our fate.

He's got to be a Number One;
an Oxford or a Cambridge Don
who'll undertake this marathon,
while we sit round, and wait.

Of course, it also could be she,
this holder of a Ph.D.
For nowadays you must agree
all genders are the same.

And if you dare to disapprove,
they'll see to it that you improve;
for who can be happy at one remove
from other people's thought?

Yet I remember Gustav Le Bon
Who, in a crowd, remained as one.
Gathering *truths* for his lexicon;

only to misreport.

Only So Far

'The Treasure of the Sierra Madre'
is a study of men and gold.
Two down-and-outs are inspired
by a lively prospector who's old.
His story doesn't sing its praise,
but simply states the facts.
How gold corrupts the seeker's mind,
unless the mind fights back.
And so we watch as words come true
when they realise their goal;
and one of the three, the weakest,
loses all self-control.

The lesson's lost on dreamers
of every caste and class.
For they've no commonsense
at all; whether lad or lass.
Take a story once in fashion,
when children everywhere were told.
that where a rainbow touched the earth,
they'd find a crock of gold.

Yet now with rockets and satellites,
so full of self-esteem,
we've set about remaking man:

though robots

never dream.

Open Gates

When one thing is another,
and you've no Wizard's hat.
That magical progression
will only leave you flat.
The Present doesn't suit at all.
The Future's fate is cast.
And so you spend each precious day
in memories of the Past.

and yet we daily met the new;
explored the world like Drake and Cook.
A little shy, but willing to try;
despite the stab of a sharp rebuke.
Retreating then to sigh and sulk,
unworthy once again.
Audaciousness with no reward,
except the mark of Cain.

But open gates allow the Fates
entry to old and new.
And once begun, a world is won
and one we'll never rue.
For then, ah then, it's once again
that magic's all around;
and butterflies enhance the skies,
now fearful days
have gone to ground.

Orders Is Orders

Big Brother's fixed in every head
filtering information.
Watching while we eat our bread,
because that's his vocation.

Guardian of all both loved and lost:
Gaoler and Warder beside.
Stiffer than any real Jack Frost
filled with formaldehyde.

"Orders is orders." You'll feel him say,
the moment he's decided.
And from then on there's no delay;
though the choice may be misguided.

He's not all there at the best of times,
and frequently gets us in trouble,
with silly tricks and pantomimes
where cauldrons bubble and bubble.

So who is he, this big, big guy
who's watching all we do?
Cyclops with his single eye?
Some tough old buckaroo?

He's none of those you might have guessed.
For I've tried to make it plain.
And now at the end, it's time to rest:
Big Brother's our

'Idiot Brain.'

Pater, Peccavi

For every minus, there's a plus,
and opposites attract.
So don't just sit around and cuss:
This law of life's a fact.

Admittedly, mathematicians say,
(those of the didactic sort.)
that adding together one and the other,
invariably leaves us with nought.

But nothing can come from nothing:
as Old Etonians used to repeat.
Recalling lessons in Latin;
and memories bittersweet.

Amo, amas, amamus
Chance meetings in the quad.
Evenings spent together,
with chaps from the Rugby squad.
. . .
Surely this meant something?
Yet still you have nothing to say.

And a minus plus a minus

means there'll be the devil

to pay.

Photography

When using words
we think we know
exactly what is what.
And so believe
we're in control;
when obviously,
we're not.
As King Canute
showed long ago;
ordering
the sea to retreat.
And sat and waited
for it to obey.
But was left
with two wet feet.

For the words we use
are in relations
that lead us
all astray.
Subject and predicate,
actor and action,
in an invisible
play.

Determination is all it takes;
but lethargy's
content with aches.

Questioning Answers

When all I've thought
has come to nought,
and I'm denied my thinking.
Will there be peace?
Will troubles cease
as the winter
Sun is sinking?

Or is it true,
I'll be born anew,
in other shapes and sizes?
To start again
as a different strain,
in a host
of new disguises?

No memories
in either case
are waiting there
for me to embrace.
Nor warmth of any
comfort zone
to help me face
new worlds alone.

But knowing now,
what lies in store
shows possibilities
I can't ignore.

For when similarities
start recurring,
chances are lessened
for future erring.

Enabling choices,
extempore.
Directions uncertain,
but fiddle-de-dee!

What will it matter
when I'm
not
me?

⟶⟨⊙⟩⟵

Rainbows

A rainbow is the metaphor
for every poem I write.
Like Edgar, and the '*Nevermore*'
that all of his poems unite.

United in mythologies
of peoples far and wide.
But varying in meaning,
as fully justified.

In Genesis, a rainbow appears
after the world-wide flood.
As a covenant made with believers,
there'd be no more shedding of blood.

As a Norseman's bridge to the heavens
or a messenger from the sky;
An archer's bow or a serpent,
the rainbow will always be high.

And up is good, and bad is down
Good news to those who wear a crown.

But not for others

about to die.

Real Faith

Was Jesus right
when he said that wrong
was only a passing madman's song?
Adopted by others to keep control;
sitting in judgement of body and soul?

Was Jesus wrong,
and the Bishops right
to choose the Dark instead of Light?
When the Church itself began to kill
Cathars who denied its will?

Holding views
that all believed
at odds with the 'Truth', as then conceived.
The Pope began a long tirade:
"A Holy war, a new Crusade.

Noblemen who
conquer these lands
will find, by chance, it stays in their hands."
And so began the twenty-year scourge
that Cathars knew as the *demiurge*.

A holocaust
and genocide
of those believers who denied
the Catholic Church and its preaching,
as contrary to Jesus' teaching.
The embodiment
of the spiritual,
being sanctified by a ritual.

Remembering Freud 1

Six years after Jekyll and Hyde
unsettled the British Isles.
A lecturer from Austria
copied its wicked wiles.
Widely published himself by now,
and happily married to boot.
A member of the bourgeoisie,
conservative to the root.

But overnight these values changed,
as shown in papers he wrote.
Previously compact and lucid,
they now had little to quote.
Exhilarated, then depressed
he swung from mood to mood.
Hated old friends, while admiring others;
the bad, instead of the good.

He pondered the myth of the hero;
and the mission to which he was bound.
Tightened his grip on his followers,
by rooting out doubters he found.
From Dr Jekyll to Mr Hyde:
How had it come about?
Headaches were the physical source,
and the cure, the cause without doubt.

Familiar with a new wonder drug
he sought to ease his pain.
And when it proved effective,
the lecturer praised cocaine.
Sniffing it through one nostril
with access more direct.
But lasting relief escaped him,
as the drug had no respect.

And so addiction was the price,
he'd pay to conquer future fame.
From then, until his final day:
when Sigmund Freud went up in flame.

Remembering Freud 2

Academically very clever,
determined to be the best;
he studied with Charcot in Paris,
embracing his methods with zest.
Psychology new, and exciting
opened a vista so wide.
The mind and all its mysteries;
a realm over which to preside.

He set up a private practice
following his return,
with patients suffering hysteria,
and so began to learn.
In a later book he cited the case
of a patient, *Anna O*
who hypnotized, revealed the pain
she'd felt some time ago.

And cured then, enjoyed her life;
a tale to fortify.
Except for one small detail:
the 'facts' had been a lie.
Neurosis wasn't the cause of her pain,
the seat of her unease.
She suffered still at treatment's end:
from a physical disease.

And no, this wasn't an error,
but a way to secure a goal.
The goal of becoming a hero;
of being in total control.
Even biographers fell into line,
when later, the myth, intact,
taken-for-granted by one and all,
was swallowed once more, as 'fact'.

Remembering Freud 3

And Freud himself ignored the lie;
at last he'd found the measure.
The key to the secrets of the brain;
by means of cocaine's pleasure.
Too happy then to realise
his thoughts were but a charade;
and happiness a delusion:
the full price yet to be paid.

For when addiction took a hold,
neurotic symptoms grew.
And the Doctor analysed himself;
hoping to make a coup.
Publishing findings in a book
exploring the world of dreams,
well received, though not by all,
who questioned sexual themes.

But then, at last support arrived
to help a comrade in need.
Four Jewish physicians joined the cause,
and with their help he'd succeed.
Others joined as years slipped by;
including Carl G. Jung.
Psychoanalysis grew by bounds;
but was it a cure, or con?

Devotees worked extra hard to spread
their master's holy word.
Repeating an ancient story
that each of us has heard.
The tale of a hero's adventures,
so easy to comprehend:
From the call, to the final battle
when the dragon is slain at the end.

Remembering Freud 4

But Anna O's dragon, remember,
lived on until she died.
So what happened to the hero
who should have been by her side?
The brotherhood protected him
as cults so often do,
from the Catholic Church of yesteryear
to Scientology's deadly brew.

And what of Freud addicted still,
though spinning webs of names.
And weighting them down with fantasy
to justify his claims.
He died in 1939, an exile
at the last. But stayed behind
in heart and mind,
the Future fed by the Past.

No scientist, by modern standards,
but still a man of worth.
His followers right in this regard
though short of any mirth.
For even he enjoyed a spree
of childishness and play
with a book that rested on the joke:

after leading us all astray.

Returning

My wife said: 'John, come see the sky."
But took offence at my reply: "I saw it yesterday."
"It's changed since then," she yelled and cried.
On cue, though new, to the funny side,
and the joy to be had from play.

For forty years we've been a pair,
like Ginger Rogers and Fred Astaire.
Yet could not dance for pain.
We both liked gardening, and I played darts,
though, most of the time, in fits and starts.
Our lives had become a bane.

So we returned to happier days
when fun and laughter meted our praise,
after the end of war.
When stars were bigger than the biggest screen
and glamour and talent reigned supreme.
Like Olympian Gods in days of yore.

And gradually found it changed us too;
that all, once old, had become the new
and sorrowing over, misery gone.

For children

at home,

in Avalon.

Ringing The Knell

Out in the field of battle
Chivalry's passed away.
Showing concern for the enemy
belongs to another day.
Remember Christmas 1914
when friend and foe both joined in sport?
How, afterwards, this carried on,
though High Command gave no support.

Yet both were against the other,
exactly the same as it was before.
Shooting with heads and feet, not guns;
but just as keen to win this war.
Their Captains shaking each other's hand
and saying: "May the best team win."
The referee's whistle familiar, but now
a signal for the game to begin.

It's a pity that Generals weren't invited.
For then they'd have seen a proper War;
with many a chivalrous gesture
that helped the hearts of players to soar.
Soldiers aware of how to behave;
following Commandments they all knew well.

While *Sopwith* and *Rumpler* waggled their wings;

leaving their comrades to ring the knell.

Roundabout

All year round at Estes Park
elks are to be seen.
Sunning themselves quite peacefully,
needing no quarantine.
Until September rolls around
and testosterone comes surging
through the bodies of virile bulls;
the product of Nature's urging.

Territorial, they'll stake their claim
and defend it against any foe.
With the twenty cows in a bull's harem
critically watching the show.
But bull against bull isn't all they'll see:
there's bull against automobiles.
Bull against bikes and visitors
clutching at driving wheels.

It doesn't concern old-timers
safe at the movie show.
Enjoying the comfort of memories
experienced so long ago.
Sitting content,
though long since spent,

knowing
what old men

know.

Scaramouche

Stewart Granger in 'Scaramouche'
wore a mask upon his face.
Pretending he was someone else,
to win himself breathing space.
Freedom to better his skill with the sword
and revenge his best friend's death.
Freedom to gain the girl he loved
and finish with ancient shibboleths:

Privilege, Feudalism, Equality for some.
Himself half nobleman by birth;
and yet at heart in sympathy
with those who called for equal worth.
Not knowing who his father was,
but told, the Count of Gavrillac.
He falls in love on meeting Aline,
only to find he's way off track.

For Gavrillac is a name that's cursed
when common to lovers both.
Since no-one in the Catholic Church
would ever befoul a Holy Oath.
But worse was to come when his friend Philippe
died by the sword of Noel de Mayne.
And André outclassed, escaped with his life
determined now to see Noel slain.

He'd need somewhere to give him cover,
but offer the grace of freedom as well.
And the building ahead, '*Commedia dell'arte*'
stood there as if by a Wizard's spell.
Opening a door, he stepped inside,
and was hit by the stench of alcohol.
And then, the familiar voice of Lenore
edged with its usual vitriol.
"Scaramouche! Drinking again!
Why I bother, I just don't know.
You drunken clown, where are you now?
Hurry. It's nearly time for the show."
And in reply, a pitiful moan
came from a nearby traveller's chest.
And Lenore, catching sight of André Moreau,
was smitten by feelings she'd long suppressed.

Closeness restored, they quickly succeeded.
Scaramouche, drunk, was left to doze.
While André absorbed Lenore's instructions,
then dressed himself in the other man's clothes.
Confidence grew as he drew on the mask.
For this was the perfect disguise.
One Scaramouche was the other's twin;
and theatre the place for telling lies.
With Lenore's advice and a natural flair
André's performance brought forth no scorn;
but peals of laughter and loud applause.
And Binet smiled:
a star had been born.

André a hit, had now the time
to sharpen his skill and kill his foe.
And Doutreval teaches him well;
until de Mayne makes a sudden show.
Enraged, forgetting all he's learned,
André's anger leads only to pain.
But certain death is pushed aside,
when a secret panel saves him again.
And now bereft of a fencing master,
Perigore of Paris becomes his aim.
Persuading Binet to move to the city
where he'll make more money to greater acclaim.
Though of course, there's never a word
of the National Assembly, set to contain
Republican deputies and Aristocrats.
Among them of course, Noel de Mayne.

But men may think that they're in charge,
while merely puppets moved by strings.
So André Moreau and Noel de Mayne
were kept apart by underlings.
Aline and Lenore, ward and lover
at work, but always out of sight.
Manipulating times and places,
and each enjoying their own delight.

But other *Aristos* in the National Assembly,
keen to challenge, with Noel away.
Eagerly insulted André;
rueing it only on duelling day.
For Perigore had calmed the temper.
Impetuosity now was gone.
And such the skill of that fencing master
that man and sword were welded as one.

They'd met by chance; by chance they met,
as Noel laughed to see the show.
"This Scaramouche is just the chap
to cure our present-day woe."
But Aline, burdened by what lay ahead,
struggled to find another ploy.
This was the end, it had to be:
though afterwards, there'd be no joy.
"Ladies and Gentlemen, we're honoured indeed
to welcome tonight the Marquis de Mayne."
People applauded, and Noel smiled
but Aline held her head in pain.
"This noise is too much, please take me home."
Noel concerned, took hold of her hand.
She softly moaned as if in pain:
and finally gained the upper hand.

He saw them leaving and glanced around.
There at the side, that rope would do.
Up to the lobby in three great strides:
time for the Marquis to pay his due.
"You may turn your back on a clown, my Lord;
having witnessed a very poor show.
But what if the man beneath the mask
were your nemesis, André Moreau?"
And then revealed his smiling face
to Noel's surprise, but satisfaction.
Now was the time he had waited for;
now was the time for action.

Advancing quickly with flashing blade,
eager to be the killer;
Noel's temper started to rise
as Andre teased from behind a pillar.
But then was driven back again
down into the balcony.
Where people quickly distanced themselves,
afraid of any injury.

The slender blades crossed and clashed
with the Marquis making the play.
While André, balanced upon the edge,
skilfully kept him at bay.
A series of passes and breaking sweep
parried the Marquis' heavy thrust.
And Andre's laughter, occasioned by joy,
left Noel more than nonplussed.

André dropped down to a sofa below,
and the Marquis did the same.
The main seats, empty, beckoned beyond,
Now was the time to finish this game.

Parrying a lunge, André stepped backwards
noting the Marquis' fading strength.
Yet still his opponent powered forward;
a man who would never stay the length.
Despite his pledge to see him dead
André paused in admiration.
Such bravery and fortitude
was needed to heal a fevered Nation.

But automatically defended himself
against another madcap attack.
Stepping quickly inside the guard,
bloodying his blade with a comeback.
It only inflamed Noel's ire.
And fed a force of Berserker zeal.
But desperation counted for little
against a swordsman with nerves of steel.
With André's point against his heart,
Noel knew he was at Death's door.
But André stared, then turned away
thrusting his sword into the floor.

And later that night, in an empty theatre,
André ponders on what he has done.
He'd promised Philippe to revenge his death,
but failed to do so although he'd won.
"André." A man approaching called.
"It's such a relief to find you here."
Philippe's father shook his hand.
"You mustn't sorrow. Be of good cheer.
Philippe knew exactly what he was doing.
He paid the price, but others now
will carry the flag, and won't desist.
We'll win this fight, somehow.
And you, I know, love Freedom's cause
as Philippe once conveyed to me.
Of course, one follows his own way,
but facts prevent catastrophe.
You thought you were a Gavrillac,
but false ideas confuse the brain.
An Aristocrat indeed you are;
but your father was the Count de Mayne."

Silence. Had André heard what he'd said?
"I'm sorry, but with my son now gone ..."
"No need, my friend, I understood.
But all we can do is to carry on.

It's a mad, mad, world as well you know
and my greatest wish is to marry Aline,
But of course I'll help, as I promised Philippe.
Unless, of course; the guillotine ..."
But then he heard a familiar voice.

"Scaramouche, Scaramouche no head you'll lose,
but marry whoever you want to choose.
For me any marriage is not on the table,
but that is my choice, as long as I'm able.
But Romance and Laughter we'll still have to share;
for to us they're as common *as vin-ordinaire.*"

Science Fiction?

Does one thing cause another?
It can, but may not hold.
Time being of the essence
in turning hot to cold.

Magnets attract iron filings,
which move from place from place;
but only in certain conditions,
when in the appropriate space.

So what attracted her to me?
What filled our hearts with Grace?

As Einstein taught, we both were one.

United in Time and Space.

Soliloquy

I met a man along the way
who had an awful lot to say
about my clothes, about my hair.
Did I not know? Did I not care?
My jeans were blue, my shirt was green
and I had nothing in between.
My shoes were brown: they should be black.
T-Shirt too tight, it should be slack.

Had I put sun cream on my head?
He'd known a girl who now was dead.
She'd thought it all an affectation,
and looked so lovely before cremation.
Needing a drink, I reached for a coke.
He glared at me. "Do you also smoke?
Everyone knows who has a brain,
coke is slang for a wrap of cocaine."

By now my blood was boiling up:
and slowly but surely I drained the cup.
Without a word, the trap was sprung.
He didn't speak. He held his tongue.
I'd silenced him by simply rebelling,
and felt my independence swelling.

No more. No more
would I let him reign.
Nor listen to
my Self again.

Snow

When I awoke in '47
and drew the curtains apart;
outside there lay a gift from heaven,
exciting my mind, thrilling my heart.

The world had changed by God's demand
and all around was new.
No more the long-neglected land,
that strangely, was taboo.

Something Near To The News

Something near to the News
is what I'm watching today.
Celebrities in abundance;
earning some extra pay.
While '*experts*' overwhelm me
in their own ineluctable way,
by ignoring Anglo-Saxon,
and switching to, Mandalay?

Are peoples' lives so poverty-stricken,
distractions like these are needed?
It brings to mind 'The Time Machine'
and the *Eloi*, superseded
by *Morlocks* living underground,
who killed, and ate them as they pleased:
even the women, who pleaded.

No Morlocks in the BBC,
but many who use duplicity
to con those waiting to hear the News.

Advertising future programmes,
solemnly waiting in snaking queues.
Eager to boost their ratings;

and pay fey producers,

their pitiful dues.

Speaking Out Loud

Speaking out loud is not for me.
I much prefer the company
of silence all around.

And only then begin to thrive,
when realising I'm alive
and ever homeward bound.

As a youngster, competing in a race,
I always hungered after first place;
ahead of all the rest.

But now I couldn't care a fig
My ego's small, Humility big;
as friends will all attest.

Although their number's becoming fewer,
I hope that some will still endure
to visit me at my end.

It's not that I've become suspicious,
or thinking thoughts that seem malicious,
that's not what I intend.

No, no. That will not do all.
I wouldn't want to disenthrall
impressions I have made.

My modesty does not permit
an ending that's indefinite:

excepting, this charade.

Special People

There are lots of ways to write a poem;
for each is of a kind.
Uniquely fashioned until at best,
then carefully refined.

Ancient or modern, happy or sad,
of every shape and size.
Poems are often serious;
playing it straight, though in disguise.

Packed with facts to please the dons
and mystify their readers.
Esoterically number one,
yet more a laggard, than leader.

But when the whip of Criticism
scourges their silky skins,
though they may strive,
not all survive
to live as paladins.

For Ying is Ying,
and Yang is Yang.
Distinct, though in relation.

And both converse without a bang:

Or fear of subjugation.

Structures

Is an invalid
invalid?
The Romans would say, yes.
For *'Validus'* in Latin
means 'strong', or 'brawniness' .
So 'weak' must be its antonym;
although we count it less.

language is not what it used to be
yet English is still at the top
the *lingua franca* of the World
with many a malaprop
speeding along to grammar's end
without a single full stop

Spelling and Speaking,
brother and sister;
who once were greeted
with great renown.
Had both their reputation's shattered:
as syntax and sense came tumbling down,
causing confusion in London town.

Standards everywhere were dropping.
Even the Censor threw in the towel.
The use of numbers instead of letters;
comedians whose jokes were foul.
Yet won applause, and screams galore
from teenagers of forty four.
Remembering Romans at the Games;
ever in need of more and more.
Blood, excitement, sights obscene;
prompting an even louder roar.
With one man armed, and the other not.
What to do but start the race?
But then, when caught and slaughtered;
the victor, disarmed, took the dead man's place.

Seneca lamented the Games' demise;
the loss of skill, courage and pride.
For spectacles of enormous size
to keep the plebeians satisfied.
A satisfaction that knew no bounds
as Roman power ebbed away.
And foreigners held back fierce tribes,
while still awaiting last month's pay.

They may seem small to those at home:
Money, clothes, and wine to drink.
But if they fail, week after week,

soldiers begin to think.

Taking Control

Inside my head the brain that's me
is waiting, waiting impatiently
to start another day;
while here I sit, at breakfast's end,
trying hard to comprehend
how he, to my dismay,
now interferes in what I eat;
which cereal, what cut of meat.
And even alters the breakfast bell
to change our eating habits as well.

It used to ring at eight fifteen,
for then we both obeyed routine,
knowing what was to come.
But now each day is so chaotic
because his moods are more despotic;
and all's *ad libitum*.
Though some would call it tit for tat,
since cooking meant a bigger hat
was needed to fit an expanding brain
that marked the start of his ragged reign.

Neurologists say the brain is me,
and minus the body, wouldn't be.
When all that's needed is bonhomie,
and change of words from 'he'
to 'we'.

The Invisible Man

Most of us are invisible
in this whirligig world of ours.
Though we thrive on communication:
Friendliness gradually sours.

Cities are much to blame for this,
mushrooming bigger and bigger.
Attracting more of the brainwashed young,
who still possess some vigour.

I'd rather be on a country road,
treading an easy pace;
welcoming fellow ramblers,
with a smile upon my face.

Though yesterday at the seaside
as I walked along the sand,
father and child came towards me,
with love and laughter at hand.

She sang a song familiar
in a voice of heavenly bliss;
that angels themselves couldn't better
despite all artifice.

I smiled at her father, and he smiled back;
free of both fetter or chain.
And continued on, passing her by:

Unseen, but renewed once again.

The Joy Of Cycling

'*The 39 Steps*' with Kenneth More
shows cycling as it used to be.
A trip into the countryside
with sandwiches and flasks of tea.

"Have a good time." They used to say.
The old folk as we passed them by,
with haversacks upon our backs:
and rain-proof capes to keep us dry.

No helmets then, no High Viz clothes;
no bicycles costing the earth.
No sunglasses needed to see the road;
just exercise, banter and mirth.

When bikes were used to carry coal
to keep the dancing fires alight.
As we huddled together in one room
at five o'clock on a winter's night.

When fathers pedalled off to work,
their trousers clipped to prevent a snag.
Smoking a Woodbine on the way;
bait box snug in their saddle bag.

No helmets then, no High Viz clothes,
no health and safety laws in place.
And yet they lived, and loved and laughed,

when common sense
had breathing space.

The Magic Of 'Shane'

We knew the pictures were only pretence,
but craving for heroes was so immense
after the Second World War;
there wasn't a boy who didn't want more.

Giants at ease on the silver screen:
fast on the draw, but never mean.
Wholesome, handsome, devil-may-care;
spawn of America, ready to dare.

But not as a man with a gun for hire.
The ruthless killer, hard to admire,
until he dies, foiling the plan
of a bitterly twisted, evil man.

On screen again, a civilian restored.
An officer once, but now deplored
by keen detectives, none too bright,
determined to prove their *facts* are right.

Always singing the same old song,
even though witnesses proved them wrong.
Until they finally had to yield,
when one confession cleared the field.

And then in Nineteen Fifty Three,
the man, the actor, unity.
Apotheosis yet again;
but this time by the name of 'Shane'.

A drifter at first, reluctant to stay;
until eventually, giving way.
Yet knowing he is doomed to roam,
even with this: the promise of home.

But not for homesteaders taking a chance,
on lawful promises, denied by the stance
of cattlemen willing to break the law:
but would they attack a family of four?

Marion the mother, Joey the son;
father, Joe Starrett, and Shane with his gun.
Even their neighbours, wary at first,
ventured the odds might soon be reversed.

He'd fail of course, and rouse their ire.
Was this stranger worth his hire?
Joey listening, knew it was, yes.
Marian silently, smoothed her dress.

And Alan Ladd beginning to doubt
how this scene was panning out.
Stevens' direction impressed him, yet
was this the part they'd both regret?

Uncertainty, that ogre of old
wasn't a beast to be controlled.
Especially not when make believe,
related directly to the word, deceive.

Yet in doing so, this reaction
was merely one of dissatisfaction.
Remedied, by calling the halt
of a common-to-all, inbuilt default.

So Shane survives his made up lies:
a hero still in Joey's eyes.
Eagerly watching, and quick to act
when seeing his hero being attacked.

Joey's the Future and Shane, the Past;
though both in the Present, will last and last.

Delighting all those who witness again,

the magical story

of

'SHANE'.

The Price Of Birth

If the puzzle of life's giving trouble,
and knots in your head force a stop.
My response is to answer in double.
But don't think of this as a prop.

It is rather a gift here presented,
after so many years of thought,
as a token for those discontented
to bring their confusion to nought.

But don't think me philanthropic.
No. No. I deplore fellow men
They're arrogant, rude, idiotic;
and I'll say so again and again.

For what's upsetting most of all
is why they cannot see beyond
themselves; making their world as small
as any stagnant pond.

Rise up! Rise up! We're but a dot:
a dot of little worth.
Despite the pain, it matters not,
for that's the price of birth.

And being so, we need to grow;
not shrivel up complaining.
For the only truth we'll ever know
is life's beyond explaining.

The Way I See It

The way I see it, worries me,
though you may answer, fiddle-de-dee;
placing your hand upon my brow,
and any fever disavow.
Shaking your head as if perplexed,
while wondering what's coming next.

The way I see it's not the same
as it once was, when I'd declaim
a judgement, as if carved in stone.
Yet now, remembering, bemoan,
while labouring, a one-eyed youth,
under a spell I held for Truth.

Ignorant, I knew it all;
though life itself held me in thrall.
Hormones demanding to have their way,
eagerly, instantly, day after day.
And Childhood, lost in hidden places;
though still at large in inner spaces.

Now all that's by, and freedom reigns,
it's back to toys, soldiers and trains.
Vision restored and body defeated,
Let's hope it's never to be repeated.

Once is enough, under the Sun;
the circle's completed,
as living's
begun.

Those Were The Days

The rules that governed who we were,
taken for granted by one and all
weren't carved in stone, but people knew
exactly who was who.

Never questioning why it was;
whether decreed by man or God.
But following rules each day,
with nothing more to say.

Babies taken away from home
at five years old, to infant schools.
Delivered by mothers near despair,
who knew at least why they were there.

Not so the children who hadn't been told
and stood like statues, watching the rest.
Too frightened on unfamiliar ground
to move a limb, or make a sound.

Until a whistle's shrilling blast
announced Authority's presence at last;
meaning order would prevail.

And far-flung Empires

never fail.

'To Be, Or Not To Be . . .'

Today my 'Stars' say plus and minus,
like a coin upon its edge.
Displaying heads and tails together,
but leaving me out on a ledge.
Which way to jump? Which way the best?
I wish I had a notion.
But Reason doesn't stand a chance
against a body in motion.

For fishes two are who I am;
pulling in both directions.
And never give a thought to me,
for I'm not allowed objections.
The stars have always been my guide,
they offered a presence secure.
But now the nearness of the moon
has made those convictions unsure.

And yet, and yet, uncertainty
is itself a Piscean trait,
and so could be a positive sign.
But that I'll have to contemplate.

'To be, or not to be,
that is the question,'

Can anyone favour me
with a suggestion?

To Seaham's Loveliest

Here's to a Lady
Sweet and gentle.
Feminine to the very core.
Not one habit
Detrimental:
She'd make a fine
Ambassador.
Heads rotate
When she's out shopping.
Women jealously stand and glare.
Even her name
Declares her 'Topping':
Blessed by a loveliness
Age can't impair.

So here's to that lady
Elemental.
A goddess of the sea and shore.
She of beauty fundamental:

I only wish

She'd paid me more.

Tomorrow's Another Day

Protestants once were Catholics,
and Pagans a while before that.
When no-one quite knew,
just who was who;
and babies were always begat.

Humans once were monkeys,
at least so Darwin says;
but very soon may be robots;
one never knows these days.

For life has changed so much, so much
since everything began;
that nowadays we have the choice
to be a woman or a man.

Or both, perhaps, at different times,
however the mood might take us.
For Science is our magic now;

and able to make

or break us.

Two Of A Kind

My reptile brain
is such a pain,
and isn't very smart.
Older than me,
we seldom agree:
are joined, but live apart.

He's rather proud
when I've been cowed;
his boisterousness excessive.
And if I say,
That's not the way,
He can be quite aggressive.

I know old age,
at anchorage,
is more than content with languor.
And by and by;
it may apply,
to calm his fits of anger.

Yet it puzzles me
continually,
just why he has to scold.
When water born,
he's filled with scorn.

With blood, that's always cold.

Waking Up

Theresa's under the microscope,
she's got that haunted look;
being beset by media wolves
she normally would not brook.

These scavengers thinking the time is ripe,
and if not now, then soon;
have never known their prey escape;
not by a Hunter's moon.

Already enjoying the taste of success
on tongue, in mouth and mind;
they snarl at each other as if at prey,
for that's how they've been designed.

And they must be act as they've been made
And we must do so too.
As little children of any age,
are partly old and new.

But no-one knows our secret Self.
So well and truly hidden;

that forms the one essential core,

and stirs itself unbidden.

Wanting More

Wanting more than what we're got
is every living thing's fatal lot.
From microbe to mammoth-sized orca whale.
It's something that we can't curtail.

Scientists warn, it'll be our end.
They're right enough. I'll not contend
the veracity of rational thought.
Modernity's powerful juggernaut

that side by side with experimentation
has won undying admiration.
Dispersing mythology, and charlatans' guile
once rendered invisible by masterful style.

But now laid bare to one and all
by cameras and microphones exceedingly small.
Confirming technology's superior worth
against the senses given at birth.

But before we bow, admitting defeat,
and wrap ourselves in a winding-sheet.

Consider this; unmentioned before.

We'd all be dead,
if it wasn't for

more.

Watch The Birdie

Take some isolated thing,
then make some connections.
Watch it soaring on the wing
in twenty nine directions.

Not only Phoenixes rise from fires,
after being reborn again.
Labels and signs still have desires,
that poets at once enchain.

For they have need of all the breed,
as well as those of figures;
preferring those unpedigreed,
to better withstand the rigours.

Yet sly remarks when at a reading.
Anonymous letters to magazines.
The skeletal result of underfeeding:
that every morality contravenes.

But that's the life our living brings;
black moods of consternation.
While Phoenixes rise on new-found wings;
to the heights of exultation.

One name embracing thousands of years,
while others are counted in legions.
The dancing bees with fancy airs
wagging their nether regions.

It's not the happy medium
by which this world is turned.
Nor Harlequin's comedian:

But the Phoenix so readily burned.

What Day Is It?

What day is it today?
I ask myself, and panic.
WHAT DAY IS IT TODAY?
As if aboard '*Titanic*'.
Though safe at home,
and breakfasting;
retired from work at last.
Freed from strife
for the rest of life,
though Time's running rather fast.

What day is it today?
Once it was automatic.
Five days on, two days off.
The formula, axiomatic.
Except when influenza raged,
rearing its ravening head;
when the Doctor called
and took one look,
then ordered me to bed.

What time is it today?
Time for a last assault.
While minutes are ticking away,
changing everything back to default.
For after all, it doesn't matter
what day it is that ends the chatter,
and brings one's heart
to a halt.

When Need Be

Big is important,
small is not.
Cold is unfriendly,
passion is hot.
Life without Wisdom
is a boat without oars.
Magical, magical
metaphors.

One thing's another
with a wave of the wand.
Abracadabra
we're here, and beyond.
Reality shimmers,
then finds itself home;
mono is changed
to polychrome.

Carpets flying
without any sails
are prominent
in Arabian tales.
As metaphors,
they've little power.

But comes the need,

then comes

their hour.

Winners And Losers

Put yourself under the microscope
if you want to win this prize;
and be prepared for the ruthlessness
you'll have to exercise.
For then you'll know what needs to be done
to alter the status quo,
and reach the heights you're aiming for:
the only way to grow.

A sculptor takes a piece of clay
and fashions it into art.
And anyone can do the same
to themselves: but first, must make a start.
And then continue, step by step
with many a tear, but nary a smile.
Until their clay, day after day
attracts admirers of Style.

But those too weak to reach this peak
are those who hate to serve.
And view the world as if surreal,
exciting every nerve.
A change that brings them great delight,
but never lasts the course.
For they're unhappy with themselves:
yet live
without

remorse.

Winning The Day?

Some people live anarchically,
staggering from day to day.
While others mechanise themselves:
preferring the easy way.
Knowing what they are going to do
for every moment arising,
in comfort, peace, security;
it's oh so, civilising.

At least that's how it used to be
when common sense was on the throne;
when discipline and cleanliness
was not a fad we could postpone.
When watching eyes behind the lace
were those of widows now deprived
of company day after day;
yearning to be revived.

But now the watchers are profiteers,
noting patterns as they appear.
Gathering facts, once privately owned,
which spread around could cost folk dear.
Yet not so much as the bigger spies
we welcome in with open arms.
All bearing gifts, though in disguise,
and triggering no set alarms.

The Silicon Valley behemoths,
hiring elites to bait their traps
for display on the World Wide Web;
and known to everyone, as apps.
Better perhaps than the wooden horse
found outside the gates of Troy.
Not as intrusive, and helpful too;
though really a cunning ploy.

For information is what they're after,
And this is something we can't ignore.
Interests, patterns, purchases, habits.
Places where they will likely occur.
For knowledge is power, and power's control;
as adverts appearing on screen compete.
Tailored to match individual taste,
though sometimes fatally indiscreet.

They sell it here, they sell it there
as fast as hands can hurry.
Neglecting warnings learnt when young,
for they've no need to worry.
With roses blooming everywhere,
and markets rising like ripening corn.
Celebrations every evening;
drinking Manhattans until the dawn.

Winning the day. Winning the day.
The prize of their insistence.
As hidden Greeks once had their way
in conquering all resistance.
But playing tricks on country hicks
won't last forever and ever.
And any fool could be the tool
causing threads to sever.

The Greeks were swallowed by a horse,
but Sili-CON Valley treats customers worse.
Milked like cows day after day,
(for Capitalism must have its way.)
Duped by words that say, we're friends;
though dedicated to other ends.

Solving problems so easily:

Creating them

for you,

and me.

With Or Without The Reins

It's bad enough to do the deed,
but lying, after you succeed,
is more debilitating.
Of course, it's nothing I'd call new.
For even the Bible takes note of it too,
because abominating.
Peter denied he knew the Lord,
lying, all of his own accord.
Despite the debt he owed.
For Jesus had warned what was in store:
that he'd deny Him thrice; no more,
before the rooster crowed.

But there's a chance it's all a spoof,
though lacking corresponding proof;
since no-one says a word.
Ignoring my linguistic snares,
built to catch them unawares;.
to establish lost accord.

For we have reached that crucial stage;
nearing the end of our pilgrimage,
short of a referee;
to oversee us night and day,
making certain that playing is play:
that madcap absentee.

For what we are is what we are
no matter what obtains.
And Life's a little foolishness,
with or without the reins.

Short
Poems

A Host Complains

Life's meaningful when someone's there,
boosting our ego by saying they care.

But all's awry,
after venison pie
and claret.

When they yap,
like a ill-trained
parrot.

⚘

Beauty And The Beast

The pitying look
of a lovely girl
doesn't affect
my ego at all.

I've passed the stage
of feeling sorry,
for a Self that's had
it's fill of worry.

But sing her praise
and won't abate.

Knowing Beauty's
there
to celebrate.

Beware The Ides ...

Teresa May
is here to stay.
Hooray! Hooray! Hooray!

No victory for the SNP.
And Jeremy's cross today.
With more support
all came to nought,
and he'll not have his way.

She's got more troops
than first she had,
but they won't bring her glory.
For, as from now, her enemy
is white, and rich, and Tory.

God's Wisdom

Because a blind man
cannot see,
he's more afraid
than you or me.

And yet, if God
should give him sight -
he'd open his eyes
and get a fright.

Men often moan:
"This Life's absurd."

Oblivious

to the ways of the Lord.

Here's The Lad

Here's to the lad,
but where's the lassie?
Skipping in the street?
At least that's how it used to be
when living life upbeat.

When lads were yang
and lassies yin,
and both of them content.
Accepting punishment as the price
for all their devilment.

∽∾∾

If

If opposites did not exist.
would their absence be truly missed?
If all was good, and nothing bad,
could we be happy, and never sad?

Or would our lives,
lacking the salt,
slowly,
slowly,
grind to a halt?

Love

When
suddenly
the chemistry
between
two people
converges.

Does love cartwheel
because
it's real;

or purely
because
of
the
urges?

༉

One Way Or Another

A woman always gets her man
one way or another;
for if he messes up her plan,
she still can be a mother.

Swapping Sides

Father had a heart attack,
because he overate.
Mother shared her food with us,
and never gained more weight.

He was as fat
as a well-fed cat;
and she was very lean.
And after he
had ceased to be
we sang:

'God save the Queen."

⌒⌒⌒

To Kill A King

Little by little
And daily done,
He poisons himself,
And thinks he's won
Immunity from
that deadly sting.

But there's
many more ways
to kill a King.